中英双语版

企鹅经典 名人大发现

斯坦·李

[美]杰夫·艾格斯（Geoff Edgers）◎著 [美]约翰·亨德利特（John Hinderliter）◎绘 刘巧丽◎译

Who Was Stan Lee?

U0870820

湖南科学技术出版社 小博集 BOOKY KIDS
·长沙·

著作权合同登记号：字18-2024-192

图书在版编目（CIP）数据

名人大发现. 斯坦·李：汉英对照 /（美）杰夫·艾格斯（Geoff Edgers）著；刘巧丽译；（美）约翰·亨德利特（John Hinderliter）绘. -- 长沙：湖南科学技术出版社，2025. 1. --（企鹅经典）. -- ISBN 978-7-5710-3274-6

Ⅰ. H319. 4

中国国家版本馆CIP数据核字第202401A6W9号

上架建议：科普读物

QI'E JINGDIAN · MINGREN DA FAXIAN：ZHONG-YING SHUANGYU BAN SITAN LI

企鹅经典 · 名人大发现：中英双语版　斯坦 · 李

著　　者：[美] 杰夫 · 艾格斯（Geoff Edgers）
绘　　者：[美] 约翰 · 亨德利特（John Hinderliter）
译　　者：刘巧丽
出 版 人：潘晓山
责任编辑：刘　竞
策划出品：李　炜　张苗苗　文赛峰
策划编辑：马　瑄
特约编辑：杜佳美
营销编辑：付　佳　杨　朔　周晓茜
装帧设计：利　锐
内文排版：金锋工作室
出　　版：湖南科学技术出版社
（湖南省长沙市芙蓉中路416号　邮编：410008）
网　　址：www.hnstp.com
印　　刷：三河市航远印刷有限公司
经　　销：新华书店
开　　本：875 mm × 1230 mm 1/32
字　　数：100千字
印　　张：5.125
版　　次：2025年1月第1版
印　　次：2025年1月第1次印刷
书　　号：ISBN 978-7-5710-3274-6
定　　价：22.00元

若有质量问题，请致电质量监督电话：010-59096394　　团购电话：010-59320018

目　录

谁是斯坦·李？ / 001
第一章　成长之路 / 005
第二章　使用笔名 / 018
第三章　接管公司 / 029
第四章　遇见琼妮 / 036
第五章　遭受非议 / 044
第六章　漫威诞生 / 050
第七章　蜘蛛侠 / 067
第八章　漫威电影 / 076
第九章　精神永存 / 092

斯坦·李生平年表 / 100
世界大事记 / 101

Contents

Who Was Stan Lee? / 103

Chapter 1 Growing Up / 106

Chapter 2 Becoming Stan Lee / 112

Chapter 3 The Teenager Takes Over / 117

Chapter 4 Joanie / 122

Chapter 5 Comics Under Attack / 126

Chapter 6 Marvel Is Born / 130

Chapter 7 Spider-Man / 141

Chapter 8 Movie Stardom for Marvel / 146

Chapter 9 Legacy / 153

Timeline of Stan Lee's Life / 156

Timeline of the World / 157

Bibliography / 158

谁是斯坦·李？

马丁·古德曼，纽约时代漫画公司的创始人，不知道该如何安置这个年轻人。但是这个少年是他妻子的表弟，妻子让古德曼在公司给他找个活干。于是，就这样，斯坦利·马丁·利伯在漫画的黄金年代，开始了自己的职业生涯。年幼之时，斯坦利便喜爱看漫画书，现在，他终于成为漫画世界里的一部分了！

时代漫画公司里到处都是超级英

雄。霹雳火能够用火来对付坏人。海底人纳摩能够在海底飞翔，自由呼吸，只他一人，便强如千军。美国队长最初只是一个骨瘦如柴的美术学生，但在美国政府招募他参加超级士兵项目后，他变成了超级英雄。

一开始，斯坦利只能独来独往。时代漫画公司里的画师们都有点可怕。他们都上了年纪，抽着大号雪茄，整天都大声地吼来吼去。一个从布朗克斯[1]来的十六岁少年能干些什么呢？

斯坦利会在午餐时间跑去帮餐馆送三明治外卖，为画师们打杂研墨。但他可不打算只是为人拿取咖啡，接听电话，然后蹉跎一生。他也有梦想。他是个作家。他想写剧本，梦想着自己也许有天能写出一本伟大的美国小说。

有一天，时代漫画公司的两位总编愤然离职。古德曼先生自己在休闲之余，比如午休和打高尔夫球的时候，

① 布朗克斯是纽约市的五个行政区之一，位于纽约市的最北端，曾经是纽约最穷的街区之一。

也需要人手帮他管理好公司。因此他把斯坦利叫了过去，并任命他为总编。

就是从这时开始，斯坦利·利伯开始使用自己的笔名“斯坦·李”。在接下来的半个世纪里，他在他人的协助下创造了一些在美国家喻户晓的超级英雄，包括蜘蛛侠、钢铁侠、绿巨人和X战警。斯坦·李不是唯一一个以漫画为生的人，但他是最成功的。

第一章

成长之路

斯坦利·利伯于 1922 年 12 月 28 日出生在纽约市。

他的父亲叫杰克，母亲叫西利娅，是来自罗马尼亚的移民，一家人住在一个非常小的公寓里。就像成千上万的其他人一样，他们梦想着来到美国，过上更好的生活，他们想在美国成家立业。

杰克在一家服装厂找到了一份裁剪布料的工作。他的工资很少，可工作时间却很长。西利娅则待在家里照顾斯坦。斯坦六岁时，经济大萧条开始了。数百万人失去了工作，其中就包括斯坦的父亲。

如今整个家庭入不敷出。杰克和西利娅开始相互争吵。每次父母吵架时，斯坦都十分担心。他深爱着他的父母，不希望看到父母争吵不休。

利伯一家搬到了更小的公寓里。杰克和西利娅不得不睡在客厅的折叠式睡椅上。公寓里只有一扇很小的窗户，窗户对面是一堵砖墙。

斯坦的妈妈希望他快点完成学业，这样他就可以去工作挣钱补贴家用。她督促斯坦努力学习，斯坦也不负所望，跳了好几级，这意味着他一直是班上最小的学生，因此，他有时很难交到朋友。

斯坦最喜欢的老师是小莱昂·B. 金斯伯格。金斯伯格先生很有幽默感，总是能用一个有趣的故事来说明他的观点。从他身上，斯坦学到如果故事讲得有幽默感，

大萧条

大萧条始于1929年10月29日，当时股市崩盘，导致许多银行和工厂倒闭。这是近代最严重的经济危机。失业率在1933年达到顶峰，当时有四分之一的美国人失业，找不到工作。

一提到赫伯特·胡佛总统的名字，人们就能想到当时许多人所面临的困难处境。“胡佛村”——由无家可归的人们搭建的帐篷和棚屋组成的村镇——随处可见。还有种汤被称为“胡佛汤”。

大萧条持续了将近十年。它不仅影响了美国，还影响了世界其他各国。

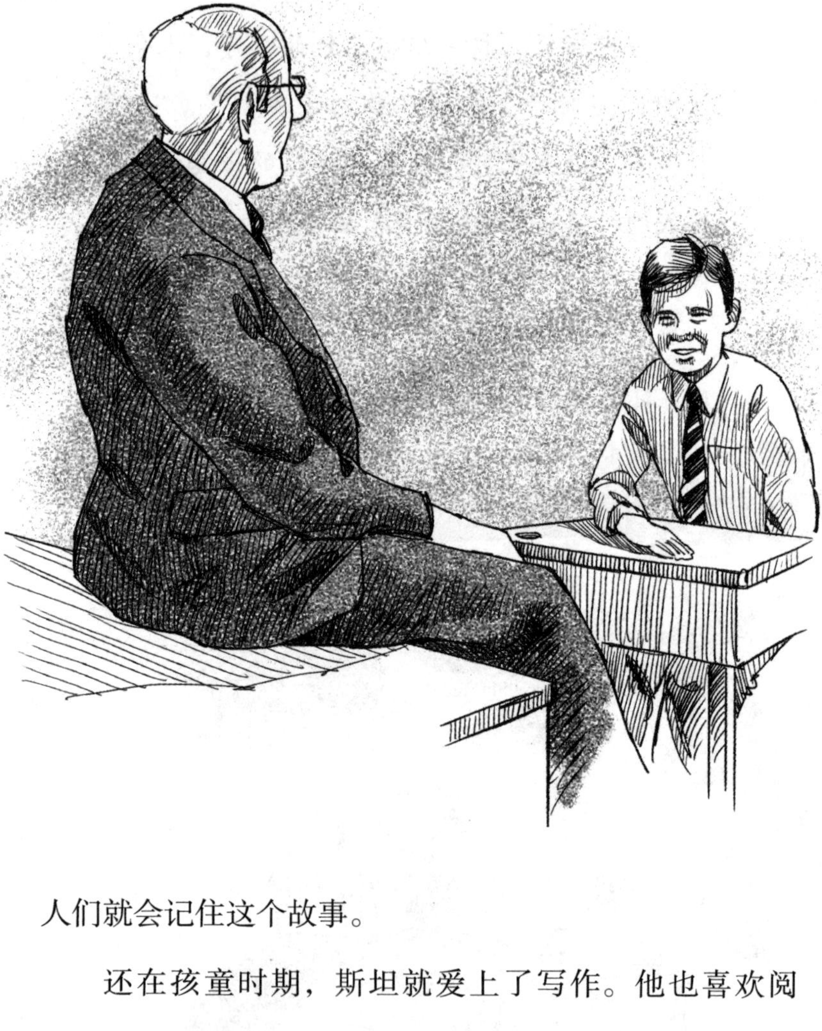

人们就会记住这个故事。

还在孩童时期，斯坦就爱上了写作。他也喜欢阅读——就算是厨房餐桌上番茄酱瓶身上的标签他也看得津津有味！事实上，斯坦在吃饭时也总是带着一本书或一本杂志。《哈迪男孩》是他最喜欢的系列丛书之一。两个爱冒险的兄弟，弗兰克和乔·哈迪，是书中描绘的两个英雄。斯坦也喜欢画画。他的画技并不高超，但这并不重要。画画帮助斯坦讲述他的故事。

夏天的时候，纽约有许多男孩去城外露营。但利伯一家没钱送斯坦去露营。于是，斯坦只能待在家里看书。斯坦的妈妈甚至给他买了一个架子，让他吃饭时也能把书立在桌子上看。

只要斯坦能买得起票，他就会去看电影。他公寓附近有五个电影院，它们会放映《科学怪人》《福尔摩斯》和《金刚》等电影。斯坦梦想成为像饰演罗宾汉的英俊演员埃罗尔·弗林那样的人。

斯坦九岁时，他的弟弟拉里出生了。随着斯坦越长越大，家里也越来越需要他出去找份工作，补贴家用。

少年斯坦最喜欢的作家

赫伯特·乔治·威尔斯（1866—1946）在英国长大，被称为“科幻小说之父”。他最著名的著作《世界之战》讲述了世界被外星人占领的故事。威尔斯写这本书的时候，人们还没有汽车，甚至还无法想象能建造火箭来进行太空旅行。

赫伯特·乔治·威尔斯

马克·吐温（1835—1910）是美国人，来自密苏里州。他的《汤姆·索亚历险记》和《哈克贝利·费恩历险记》都十分贴合人们平时的说话方式。他还写了白人是怎样对黑人持有偏见的。这在当时是革命性的。

马克·吐温

阿瑟·柯南道尔爵士

阿瑟·柯南道尔爵士（1859—1930）来自苏格兰，创造出令人惊叹的神探夏洛克·福尔摩斯。福尔摩斯抽着烟斗，和他最好的朋友华生医生一起探案解谜。

斯坦不怕吃苦，只要有工作他就接。他给报社写过稿，送过三明治外卖，做过制裤公司的杂工。

即使在工作赚钱补贴家用的同时，斯坦也一直坚持写作，并且他的写作水平渐入佳境。当地一家报社赞助了一个征文比赛。由于斯坦获奖次数太多，这家报社不得不让他停止参赛！他们希望别人也有机会获胜。但那家报社的编辑也表扬了斯坦，并鼓励他发挥自己的才能。那个鼓励对他来说意义非凡，斯坦永远也不会忘记。

第二章

使用笔名

1939 年，十六岁的斯坦从德威特·克林顿高中毕业了。和他同龄的很多孩子都在想上大学的事，但斯坦不行，他得继续工作。在他表姐琼的帮助下，他来到马丁·古德曼的时代漫画出版公司工作。

古德曼先生几乎不认识斯坦。斯坦来上班的那天，古德曼先生问："你在这里干什么？"

古德曼先生在开玩笑吗？难道琼忘了向她丈夫提起斯坦这个人？斯坦一直也没机会问，因为他太忙了。

时代漫画公司在曼哈顿出版了二十多种杂志。有些是以旧西部为背景的冒险故事，还有一些是关于科学和健康的。斯坦被分派到了公司的漫画部门。“还部门呢，”斯坦开玩笑地说，“其实就是分派到了乔和杰克的手下。”

乔的全名叫乔·西蒙。他是总编——负责所有书稿的编辑。杰克的全名就是杰克·科比。他是时代漫画公司最好的画家。这两个人对斯坦影响很大。但他们看起来并不友善。斯坦刚去的时候，他们连头都没抬。

刚开始工作的时候，斯坦只是一个“勤杂工”——老板需要什么，他就做什么。虽然他每周只能赚八美元，但斯坦并不介意。能在时代漫画公司工作，他感到很自豪。

斯坦每天来往于布朗克斯和第四十二大街的时代漫画公司办公室之间。乔和杰克工作的办公室没什么特别的。杰克会坐在画板前。乔则不时在房间里踱步。斯坦有时会开玩笑说，他们在雪茄的烟雾缭绕中消失了。

那个时候，时代漫画公司与其他漫画公司的竞争非常激烈。DC 漫画公司创作出超人和蝙蝠侠。但时代漫画公司创作出的两个超级英雄并没有那么出名。

霹雳火是在实验室里创造出来的机器人。他能从手中直接射出火焰，也可以突然变成一个火球。

漫画书是怎样形成的

制作一本漫画书一共有五个主要阶段。作家创作故事，画家用铅笔画出故事插画，然后文字雕刻员小心翼翼地将故事的文字用墨印到纸上，每个过程中，编辑都要确保漫画质量能进入下一个环节。

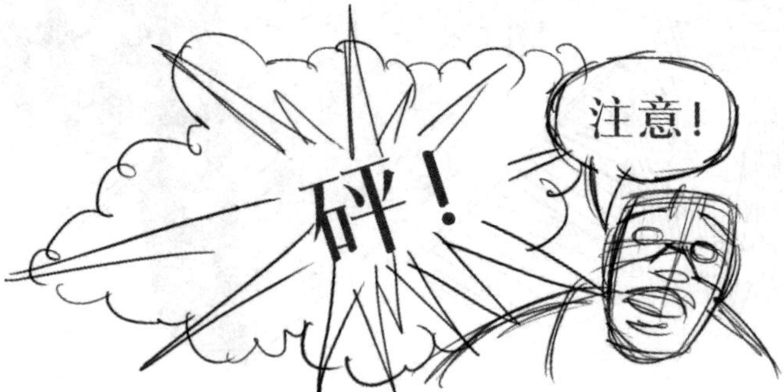

等一切都准备好后，这些漫画就会被交给油墨工。如今，人们在电脑上就可以给已经画好的铅笔画进行加工。漫画公司可以使用电脑而不是人力来节约成本。但即使到了 20 世纪 90 年代，

油墨工依然是漫画绘制过程中一个非常重要的画家角色。他或她的工作就是将铅笔插画变成富有戏剧性的黑白漫画。

对铅笔插画进行加工润色之后，漫画书就可以开始上色，之后就可以开始印刷。

但霹雳火不能一直操控这些火焰。海底人纳摩还有一个更大的问题，他是亚特兰蒂斯的公主和一位人类船长所生，但他一点也不像人类！

1940 年，乔·西蒙和杰克·科比为时代漫画公司创作了《美国队长》。此时，第二次世界大战在欧洲肆虐，西蒙和科比对他们听到的关于阿道夫·希特勒的事感到震惊。

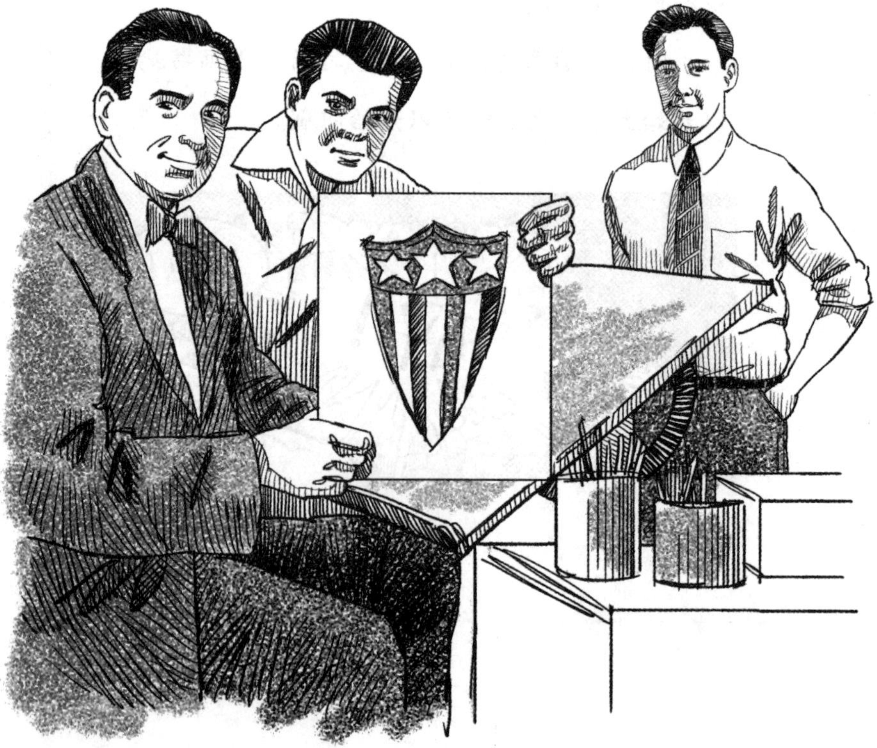

美国队长的任务是对抗纳粹德国。他穿着红、白、蓝三色的服装，与美国国旗的颜色相同。他手持的盾牌能挡住子弹。

《美国队长》一经刊发，就大获成功，卖出了一百万册。超人终于有了竞争对手！

这时，斯坦才有机会不再打杂。有一天，乔·西蒙把斯坦叫了过去。他问斯坦能不能为新一期的《美国队长》写个故事。斯坦激动极了！他写了一个故事，叫《美国队长挫败叛徒的复仇》。

对他写的第一个故事，没有多少人给予赞赏，但斯坦并不介意。重要的是斯坦马上又接到了写第二个故事的任务。

写完《美国队长挫败叛徒的复仇》之后，斯坦开始写更多的故事。写作过程中，斯坦决定不用真名，而用笔名。他考虑过给自己取名为“头条猎者”“海外特派员”“斯坦·马丁”甚至“李·坦斯”，也就是把“斯坦·李”倒过来念！斯坦不想用他的全名，斯坦利·利伯。“我准备把这个名字留给我那本伟大的美国小说呢，”他开玩笑说，“那本我一直也没动笔写的小说。”最后，他决定以后都用这个笔名——斯坦·李——姓和名都只取一半。

第三章

接管公司

随着斯坦的写作任务变多，乔和杰克的写作任务就变少了。古德曼先生左右为难。他不想给这两位画家太高的工资，他们对此也颇有微词。所以乔和杰克决定从时代漫画公司辞职。

“我环顾四周，想看看有谁可以代替他们，然后我意识到，没有人可以代替他们，”斯坦继续说，“除了我，那里只有我一个人。”

斯坦对故事有很多想法，但不会画画。所以他一直和画家们保持密切合作。他还继续担任公司的总编，虽然有时一个十八岁的少年当老板会很艰难。有时候，有人会去敲斯坦办公室的门，然后问：“嘿，孩子，李先生在哪里？”

大概在一年的时间里，斯坦经营着时代漫画公司。

古德曼先生想要他写什么，他就写什么。

他写过西部故事、悬疑故事、恐怖故事，甚至还写过一些浪漫爱情故事。尽管斯坦热爱他的工作，但他的事业还是被中断过。美国加入了第二次世界大战，斯坦想为此尽一份力量。

他决定自愿参军，并于 1942 年冬天应征入伍。

第二次世界大战

第二次世界大战是历史上规模最大的战争，于 1939 年在欧洲正式爆发。世界上每一个主要国家都参与其中，全世界有一亿人在军队服役。形成了敌对的两大军事集团：同盟国和轴心国。

1941 年 12 月 7 日，日本轰炸机突然袭击夏威夷地区的珍珠港，随后美国加入了第二次世界大战。将近二千四百名军人在那天牺牲。

珍珠港事件吓坏了美国人，但同时也激励

了他们。不少人自愿参军，漂洋过海加入同盟国（包含英国、法国和苏联），以对抗轴心国（包含德国、意大利和日本）。

尽管同盟国赢得了这场战争，但也付出了巨大的代价。在 1945 年德国和日本最终投降之前，死亡人数超过五千万，使得第二次世界大战成为人类历史上最惨烈的战争。

斯坦的正式军职是“剧作家”。由于他之前的工作经历，他在军队的时候主要是为美国政府撰写训练手册、宣传口号和拍摄训练电影。这个工作可并不多见。

除了斯坦·李，只有八个人被美国陆军归类为“剧作家”，包括电影导演弗兰克·卡普拉、小说家威廉·萨罗扬和西奥多·盖泽尔，也就是人们熟知的苏斯博士。

值得注意的是，斯坦在军队服役期间也一直在为时代漫画公司工作。公司会把想法写进信里邮寄给斯坦，他会将他写好的故事从他驻扎的地方寄给公司。

尽管斯坦愿意为国效力，但当1945年战争结束时，他还是很激动。他迫不及待地想回到充满漫画书的世界。

第四章

遇见琼妮

第二次世界大战结束后，斯坦回到纽约，再次担任时代漫画公司的总编。这份工作他做了二十五年，一直做到 1972 年，那年他成了发行人。那段时间是斯坦一生中最快乐的时光。他在艾玛纳克酒店租了一套两居室的公寓，还买了一辆白色的大轿车。这是他拥有的第一辆新车！

好事接连发生。有一个朋友想把斯坦介绍给一个叫贝蒂的模特。他的朋友认为贝蒂和斯坦会是很般配的一对。当斯坦来到模特经纪公司时，开门的是一个他所见过的最漂亮的女人。只是有一个问题：她不是贝蒂。这个年轻女孩的名字叫琼。

琼 · 克莱顿 · 布科克

琼 · 克莱顿 · 布科克留着一头红发，长了一双蓝眼睛，幽默感十足。她从英国搬到纽约，是一个帽子模特。在 20 世纪 40 年代，女性每天都戴帽子。帽子模特必须很漂亮才行。她们的脸经常出现在报纸和杂志的广告上。

斯坦不是一个善于隐藏自己情感的人。“我爱你。”他那天刚一见面就忍不住将这句话脱口而出。琼笑了。但她同意和他约会。

1947 年 12 月 5 日，斯坦和琼成为夫妻。主持他们婚礼的评定人，就是刚刚批准琼和她的第一任丈夫离婚的那个评定人！斯坦想在琼改变主意之前尽快和她结婚！

斯坦非常激动，将他美丽的新娘称为琼妮。

这对年轻夫妇搬到了离时代漫画公司曼哈顿办公室很近的一个公寓里。那地方太小了，只容得下一张床，但是斯坦和琼妮并不介意。他们晚上会和朋友一起出去跳舞。生活十分美好。

两年后，斯坦和琼搬到了纽约市外长岛上的一栋房子里。斯坦的母亲西利娅去世时，他的弟弟拉里才十五岁。他和斯坦、琼妮一起搬进了新房子。

居住空间更大了，这是一件好事！1950年，斯坦和琼生了一个女儿，名叫琼·西利娅。三年后，他们的第二个女儿简在出生几天后就去世了，这让他们伤心欲绝。医生告诉琼妮，她以后都不能再生孩子了。

斯坦很爱他们的女儿琼·西利娅。他会把她放在肩膀上，背着她在大院子里转。他将她和他们可爱的德国

牧羊犬布莱基和辛巴一起玩耍的照片都拍了下来。而且，为了有更多的时间和琼·西利娅在一起，斯坦尽量在家工作。

斯坦很高兴不用被关在时代漫画公司烟雾缭绕的办公室里，他可以在外面的阳光下工作。他把打字机放在后院的桌子上，站着工作。有时，朋友们会过来陪陪斯坦。其他时候，琼·西利娅会邀请自己的小朋友来家里做客。

当斯坦努力工作时，旁人很难不注意到他。斯坦写漫画故事的时候，喜欢把所有的字大声念出来。这有助于让他笔下的超级英雄更真实。砰！嗞！他会大声喊出所有最戏剧性的部分！

琼·西利娅的朋友有时会奇怪为什么她的父亲要发出那些声音。琼·西利娅让他们不用担心，那只是她父亲在工作而已。

第五章

遭受非议

不是每个人都像斯坦一样喜欢漫画。从 20 世纪 40 年代初开始，有一些成年人抱怨漫画书对孩子不好。为什么？因为漫画书里充满了暴力、血腥的细节和可怕的故事。人们担心漫画会给年轻人带来不良影响。

1948 年，一些愤怒的父母甚至在纽约州的宾厄姆顿和西弗吉尼亚州的斯潘塞举行了公开焚烧漫画书的活动。

1949年，非常受欢迎的《家庭圈》杂志发表了一篇题为《关于漫画书你能做些什么?》的文章，这篇文章告诉父母，他们需要在孩子看漫画之前先看一下，以确保它们是“安全的”，不会太暴力。

斯坦和其他漫画创作者并没有把这些抱怨当回事。他们的生意仍然很好。

但在1954年，儿童心理学家弗雷德里克·沃瑟姆写了一本名为《诱惑无辜》的书。沃瑟姆博士说漫画书对孩子们很危险。他的想法导致华盛顿特区举行了几场关于是否禁止漫画书的国会听证会。一些商店甚至停止向儿童出售漫画书!

国会听证会对漫画书的销量产生了巨大影响。仅1954年一年就有十五家漫画公司倒闭。

剩下的出版商尽了最大努力生存下去。他们一起创立了漫画准则管理局。

他们制定了自己的规则，以确保漫画书中不包含会让父母或政客感到不安的故事。

每本漫画书在印刷之前都要经过漫画准则管理局的批准。如果获得了批准，漫画书可以在其封面上使用“漫画准则管理局批准印章”，这表示它对孩子们来说是“安全的”。

漫画准则管理局

漫画准则管理局规定漫画书要：

· 尊重权威（如警察）。

· 确保正义永远战胜邪恶。

· 不许使用“恐怖”或“可怕”这样的词。

· 不准出现吸血鬼、狼人、食尸鬼或僵尸！

斯坦多年来一直遵守着这些准则。1971 年，美国政府要求斯坦创作一部蜘蛛侠漫画，讲述毒品和吸毒的危害。但是漫画准则管理局甚至不允许漫画书提到“毒品”这两个字！斯坦无视了这个准则，出版了三期以蜘蛛侠为主角的禁毒特刊。这批漫画没有印上“漫画准则管理局批准”的印章。尽管如此，这些漫画还是十分受人欢迎。斯坦知道他现在可以制定自己的准则了。2001 年，漫威正式退出了漫画准则管理局，并创建了自己的评判体系。

第六章

漫威诞生

到 1960 年的时候，斯坦已经从事漫画工作二十年了。但他再也没有那么开心了。漫画书不再那么畅销。相比老的超级英雄，孩子们对电视节目和摇滚音乐更感兴趣。就连《美国队长》也因为销量低而被取消印发。

斯坦不禁想起了与杰克·科比在时代漫画公司烟雾缭绕的房间里度过的美好时光。他怀念以前的团队，怀念过去上班时的那种兴奋。他告诉琼妮他要辞职。他打算冲进古德曼先生的办公室，告诉他自己不再搞漫画了。

只是出现了一个问题。

正当他准备辞职时，古德曼先生向斯坦提出了一个令人兴奋的新挑战。他们的竞争对手，DC 漫画公司刚刚推出了一本漫画书：《美国正义联盟》。

这本漫画书里不是只有一个超级英雄，而是由七个超级英雄组成了一个团队：超人、蝙蝠侠、神奇女侠、闪电侠、绿灯侠、海王和火星猎人！

“正义联盟”漫画被抢购一空。

古德曼先生让斯坦组建自己的团队。他甚至提议让美国队长和霹雳火回归。

当斯坦把古德曼先生的想法告诉琼妮时，琼妮告诉斯坦，她会一直支持他。她比任何人都了解她的丈夫。她知道他喜欢创造性的挑战。

“你知道吗，斯坦？”琼妮说，“如果马丁想让你创造一群新的超级英雄，这可能是一个机会，让你能做你一直想做的事。”

她的意思是斯坦没有什么可失去的。如果他冒着大风险惹恼了古德曼先生，他可能会被解雇。但这对斯坦来说无关紧要，因为他已经打算辞职了！但如果他能想出一些特别的东西，古德曼先生会很高兴，他也能重新找回他早年在时代漫画公司工作时的兴奋感。

斯坦不想让老角色回归。他想创造新的角色。他创造的新团队不会像超人那样英俊潇洒，也不会像美国队长那样强大无比。他们也像普通人一样，有问题和弱点。他们的生活也并不总是一帆风顺。

斯坦知道谁能够帮得上忙：他的老搭档杰克。

杰克·科比

杰克·科比出生于1917年8月28日。他十四岁时开始在艺术学校上课。不久之后，他的父亲失业了，他不得不退学。

杰克是个十分优秀的漫画家。在时代漫画公

司和后来的漫威漫画公司，杰克帮助斯坦·李创造了美国队长、神奇四侠和其他一些重要的超级英雄。别人称他为“国王”科比。但是杰克不喜欢绰号。他希望自己的工作得到认可。他认为斯坦霸占了聚光灯，自己创造了那么多角色但没有得到足够的关注，他因此而感到不满。他不明白为什么那么多文章只提到斯坦的功劳。

斯坦告诉大家，是杰克和他一起创造了这些角色。但直到 1994 年去世，杰克都觉得自己受到了欺骗，并且很多年没和斯坦说过话。

杰克·科比被认为是有史以来最伟大的漫画艺术家之一。

杰克辞去时代漫画公司的正式工作已经有好几年了。但从 1958 年开始，杰克就开始接受斯坦派给他的任务。现在，斯坦需要更多的东西。他需要杰克的帮助来创造新一代的漫画英雄。

神奇四侠由杰出的科学家里德·理查兹领导。第二位成员，苏·斯托姆，希望有一天能嫁给里德。苏的弟弟约翰尼·斯托姆是这个团队的第三位成员。但斯坦和杰克最伟大的创造是神奇四侠里的最后一位成员：

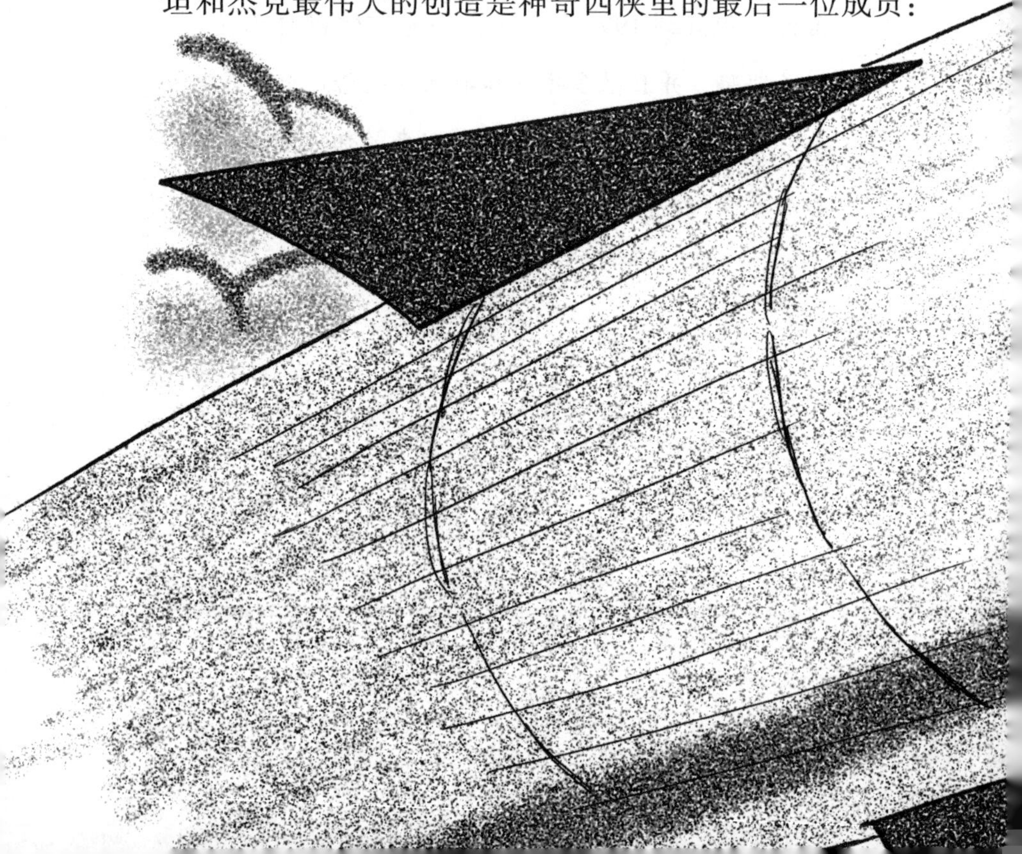

本·格里姆。他本是一位军事飞行员，是里德的朋友。

去外太空旅行是里德的梦想。他建造了一艘宇宙飞船，并邀请了本、苏和约翰尼一同前去。进入太空后，他们受到了辐射的冲击，这使得他们每个人都拥有了一项特殊的能力。

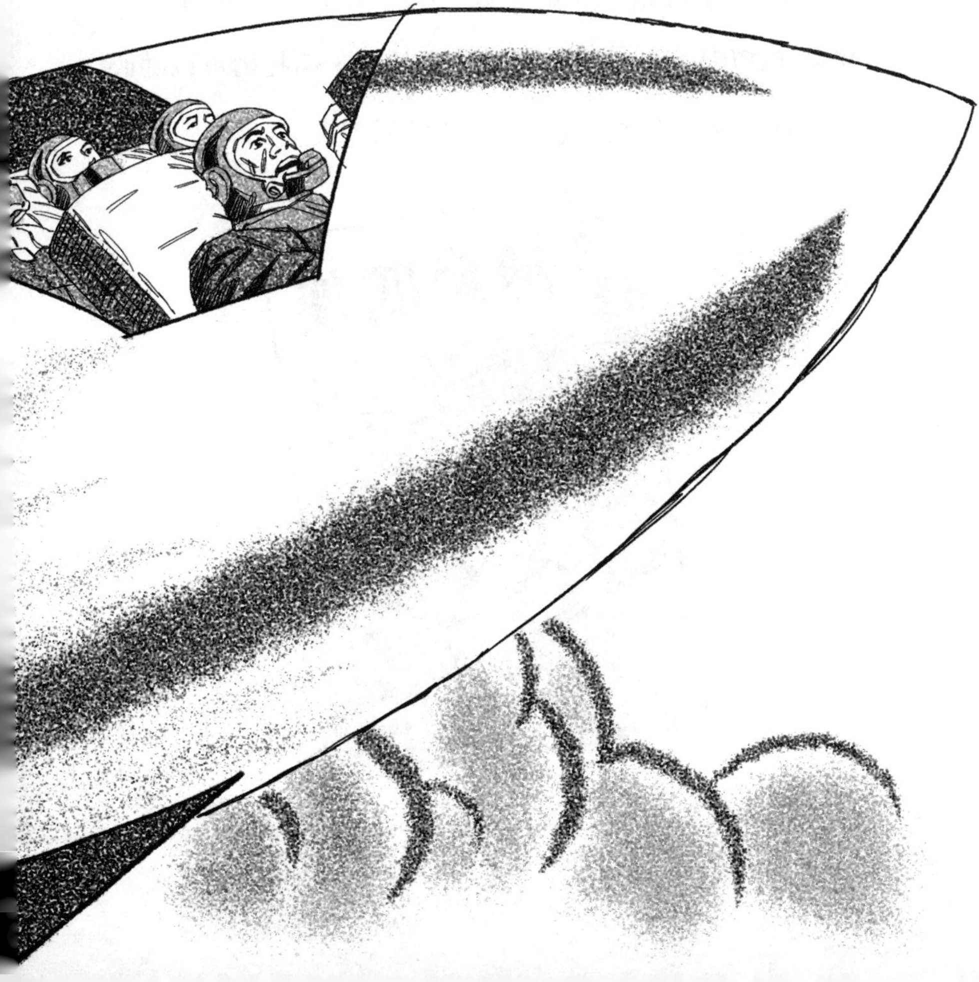

但是本的身体结构发生了变化。辐射让他变成了一个有着橙色岩石般皮肤的巨人。沮丧的本给自己改名为“石头人”。

“石头人”是一种新型的超级英雄。本嘟囔着，翻了个白眼。他希望自己能变回正常的模样。但他非常忠诚，坚信要打击犯罪。里德变成了大嘴巴的“神奇先生”。苏·斯托姆成了“隐形女侠”。约翰尼·斯托姆可以随心所欲地喷出火焰来，成了新一代的霹雳火。

1961 年，这本漫画书一经出版，神奇四侠就深受读者喜爱！

神奇四侠的成功使斯坦相信，他接受古德曼先生的挑战是正确的决定。这也给了他创造其他超乎想象的英雄的信心。

斯坦小时候就读过罗伯特·路易斯·史蒂文森的《化身博士》。这本书讲述了一个人有着两种截然不同的性格的故事。杰基尔博士是一个非常好的人，但是海德先生却是一个邪恶的人。

对新角色，斯坦想出了另一个版本的化身博士。布鲁斯·班纳博士是一位温文尔雅的科学家。但当他发脾气或感到恐慌时，他会变成一个绿色的怪物：绿巨人浩克。

1962年，绿巨人第一次出现在《不可思议的浩克》第一部中，并在漫画迷中迅速流行起来。

斯坦的下一个漫画团队是一群被抛弃的变种人，叫“X战警”。泽维尔教授，他们的导师，告诉这群变种人，他们也可以成为英雄。

斯坦的事业经营得顺风顺水，但他很忙，需要帮手。他找到了最合适的人选。他叫来了自己的弟弟拉里。拉里·利伯上过艺术学校，为斯坦写过一些故事。现在他们合作得更加密切了。在接下来的两年里，斯坦和拉里一起创造了漫威最受欢迎的两个角色，雷神和钢铁侠。

当拉里厌倦了画这些角色时，他推出了一系列西部主题作品，名叫《皮鞭小子》。斯坦则不断创造出新的角色，其中就包括超胆侠和蚁人。

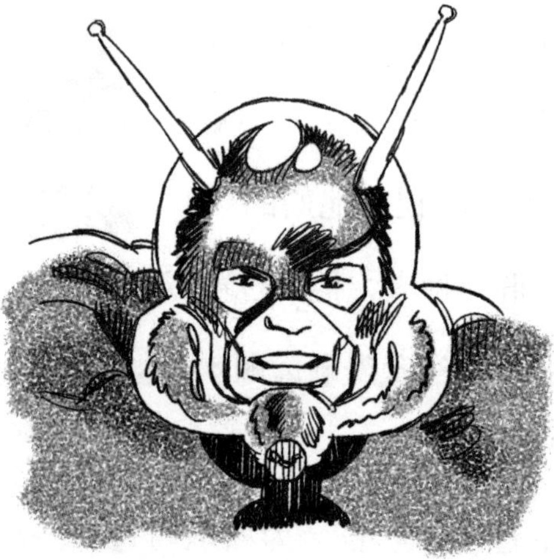

收获了这么多的成功后，斯坦决定做一个重大的改变。

20 世纪 50 年代，古德曼将时代漫画公司更名为亚特拉斯漫画公司。但斯坦认为公司需要一个更新鲜的名字。时代在变化。斯坦也正在用一种新的风格和方法去做漫画。虽然他又开始创造超级英雄，但新的一拨却有所不同。他们也会有问题！他们有时会苦于自己拥有超能力，渴望成为普通人。斯坦想起了时代漫画公司早期出版的一本漫画书使用的书名：漫威。他喜欢这个名字！古德曼也同意更名了。

斯坦给漫威漫画公司的漫画家和作家们都起了绰号，称他们为他的“牛棚”。作家、漫画家和油墨工都在漫威的主办公室里工作。斯坦想让漫威的读者把漫威想象成一个大型俱乐部，每个人都在那里闲逛、讲笑话，并且能创作出令人惊叹的漫画书。

如果读者有问题，他们可以直接写信给斯坦。他会在每本漫画书的“牛棚公告”处回复这些信。斯坦很喜欢写这些回复。他在每篇公告的页面顶部起了一个听起来很滑稽的标题，比如“你的漫威疯子为你带来的更有趣、更不朽、更令人震惊的备忘录!”。在牛棚公告处开设的专栏《斯坦的肥皂箱》里，斯坦给读者写了一封公开信，并写出了他自己最喜欢的几句话，比如“不说了!”和

“精益求精！”。

斯坦开玩笑说，其他的漫画公司都是“小鱼小虾”。漫威漫画才是王者。

欢乐漫威游行协会

漫威漫画的内部粉丝俱乐部成立于1965年2月。这个俱乐部被称为“欢乐漫威游行协会”（简称M.M.M.S.），包括Q.N.S.（神棍组）和F.F.F.（无畏的先锋）等不同的队伍。只要交一美元的会员费，俱乐部成员就会收到一封欢迎信、一张会员卡、贴纸、纽扣和一张《漫威之声》的单面唱片，里面有斯坦、“牛棚”里的家伙们和斯坦的秘书——了不起的弗洛·斯坦伯格的声音。

1969年，欢乐漫威游行协会被并入更大的漫威国际粉丝俱乐部中。

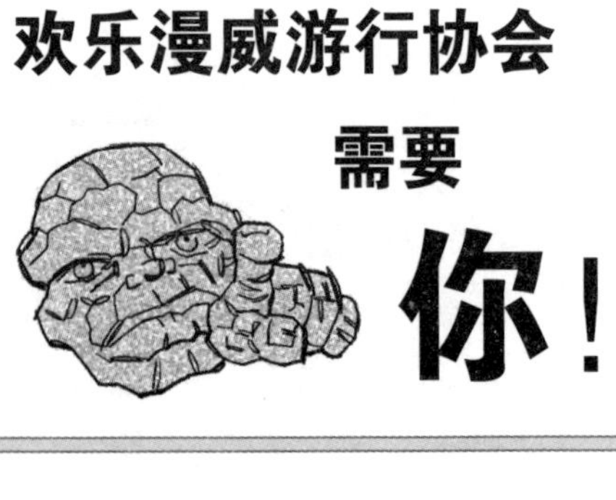

第七章

蜘蛛侠

即使公司有了新名字，取得了新的成功，斯坦也很难向古德曼解释他的新想法。谁会对一个能像苍蝇一样粘在天花板上的瘦小少年感兴趣呢？“蜘蛛侠”？斯坦难道不知道人们讨厌蜘蛛吗？

斯坦说，他是在看到一只苍蝇爬上墙后想到蜘蛛侠这个主意的。

一个能粘东西的超级英雄怎么样？斯坦绞尽脑汁想取个好名字。“苍蝇侠”或“昆虫侠”听起来都不对劲。随后，斯坦想到了“蜘蛛侠”。这名字可以！

他原本想请漫画家杰克·科比来画这个新角色，但后来觉得杰克的画不合适。杰克创造的蜘蛛侠看起来太英雄主义，太强大了。

蜘蛛侠的真名是彼得·帕克，一个不自信的宅男少年。校橄榄球队的明星闪电·汤普森更是常常在学校欺负他。彼得被一只受到核辐射的蜘蛛咬伤了后，竟然有了超能力。这个害羞的男孩突然可以粘在墙上和天花板上，就好像他的手有吸盘一样。他还超级强壮。

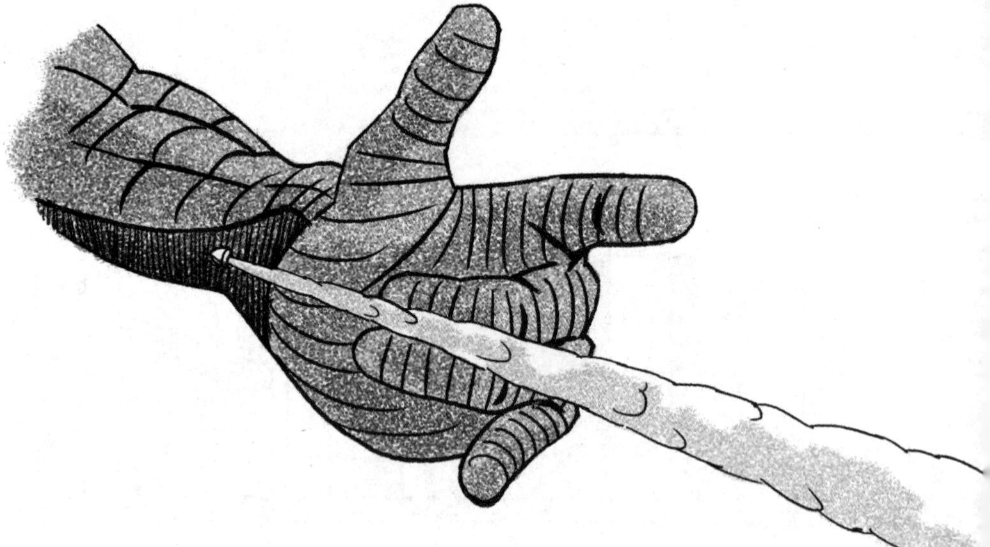

为了创造好这个新的超级英雄，斯坦找到了一个画手伙伴史蒂夫·迪特科。史蒂夫本人笨拙害羞，不喜欢参加聚会。他能轻而易举地将彼得·帕克塑造得与众不同。彼得·帕克不会是一个肌肉发达的巨人英雄。但当彼得变成蜘蛛侠时，他又变成了一个经典的超级英雄，史蒂夫给他设计了新的“造型”和服装。

史蒂夫·迪特科

蜘蛛侠于 1962 年 6 月首次出现在漫画书中，他是斯坦新思路下的完美角色：普通人碰巧成了超级英雄。漫威英雄也会有缺点和问题。但最终，他们会投身于打击犯罪的斗争中。

尽管古德曼先生心存疑虑，但第一本以蜘蛛侠为主题的漫画书还是很受欢迎。事实上，漫威推出的这群新超级英雄在1962年卖出了一千三百万本漫画书，销量几乎是前一年的两倍！

斯坦经历过20世纪40年代的“漫画黄金时代”。现在，他成了“白银时代”的缔造者之一，“白银时代”大约从1956年持续到1970年。漫画迷们有时把这种从犯罪和浪漫故事回到超级英雄的流行趋势称为“白银六十年代”，甚至是“漫威时代”。

谁说没人喜欢蜘蛛？

漫威的一些大反派

毁灭博士是一位发明家和巫术天才，他是神奇四侠的头号敌人。

行星吞噬者，来自塔星球的行星吞噬者非常强大，他可以吃掉整个星球。

绿魔是蜘蛛侠的敌人之一，是一个以万圣节为主题的超级反派，他的武器包括蝙蝠、幽灵和会爆炸的南瓜灯。

奥创的外甲非常强大。他几乎是坚不可摧的。他也是个天才。

灭霸是一个变种人，他可以用一把特殊的椅子环游太空。他用超人的力量与钢铁侠、石头人和蜘蛛侠对抗。

洛基既是雷神父亲收养的孩子，也是雷神的死敌。他的全名是洛基·劳菲森。

毒液是一种寻找人类宿主的液体状外星生物，是蜘蛛侠的宿敌之一。

万磁王生来就有特异功能。他的家人在第二次世界大战中丧生，他认为变种人也需要被保护，于是他成为一个反派。

狂攻是由X教授和万磁王的灵魂结合而成的。他同时与绿巨人和X战警为敌。

第八章

漫威电影

漫威漫画公司现在赚得盆满钵满，古德曼先生决定是时候卖掉它了。1968 年，一个名叫马丁 · 阿克曼的人买下了这家公司，但有一个条件：斯坦 · 李必须继续负责管理这家公司。

斯坦继续管理着这家公司。现在，斯坦已经是漫威的门面了。虽然那些漫画家都比较内敛，可斯坦外向的性格使他成为公司的天然代言人。他在大学和大会上发表演讲。他参与杂志和报纸的拍摄。斯坦也形成了自己独特的形象。他留着小胡子，别人一眼就能认出来，而且即使在室内他也总是戴着墨镜。

1972 年，古德曼先生正式从出版人的职位上退休。斯坦升职成了漫威的新出版人。曾参与《X 战警》创作的作家罗伊·托马斯成为漫威的编辑。作为出版人，斯坦可以专注于新想法。

斯坦希望漫威的角色能被改编到电视节目和电影中。

改编成电视节目很容易。1977 年,《不可思议的浩克》在电视上首播。斯坦不是这个电视剧的负责人，但他却十分重要。《不可思议的浩克》的制片人希望绿巨人是红色的，而不是绿色的。斯坦拒绝了。他说绿巨人必须是绿色的。《不可思议的浩克》在五年多的时间里拍了八十多集！

斯坦花了很多力气才让漫威漫画进入电影领域。多年来，电影制片人一直拒绝将漫画书改编成电影。他们用真正的演员来表现漫画中的插图动作太难了。1978年，电影《超人》上映后，一切都改变了。演员克里斯托弗·里夫扮演了超人。

这部电影在全球获得了三亿美元的票房，是当时票房第六高的电影。《超人》让好莱坞相信超级英雄电影是可以获得成功的。

斯坦开始与好莱坞制片人会面。1980 年，他和琼妮搬到了洛杉矶。

他们在西好莱坞买了一栋可以俯瞰日落大道的房子，日落大道是洛杉矶的好地段，遍地都是商店、餐馆和摇滚俱乐部。太令人兴奋了！斯坦和琼妮都喜欢好莱坞。他们在加利福尼亚结交了新朋友。琼·西利娅当过模特，随后又开始画画。她的父母第一次去看她的画展时非常激动。

尽管斯坦很喜欢加利福尼亚，但他发现拍电影并不容易。制片人们会发生争吵，互相起诉对方。有一次编剧们为电影版的《蜘蛛侠》写了八个不同的剧本。没有一个人满意。

导演詹姆斯·卡梅隆曾想拍一部《蜘蛛侠》电影。但拍摄《蜘蛛侠》十分耗时，于是他转而拍了《终结者》和《泰坦尼克号》等电影。

1989 年，斯坦拍摄了一部关于漫威角色“惩罚者”的电影，但这部电影从未在电影院上映。1994 年拍摄的《神奇四侠》也是如此。

在好莱坞的斗争着实让斯坦大吃一惊。在纽约，漫威漫画公司也遇到了问题。阿克曼在 1986 年卖掉了漫威，新东家想要扩张公司。

公司想迈的步子太大，走得太快。他们收购了一家棒球卡片公司和一家贴纸公司。收购两家公司都赔了钱。

终于，在 1996 年，漫威破产了。公司也倒闭了。

但斯坦从未放弃。他知道漫威家族的英雄总有一天会在大银幕上收获新的粉丝。他也知道漫威需要他。每个人都知道斯坦·李！为了重振漫威，新东家想出了一个计划。

他们在漫威内部成立了一个专门制作电影的部门。他们称之为漫威工作室。一个叫阿维·阿拉德的人成为该部门的负责人。

阿维·阿拉德

阿维从小生活在以色列，读着被翻译成希伯来语的蜘蛛侠漫画书长大。他很高兴斯坦能给他建议。

在阿维的领导下，漫威终于开始制作电影了。1998 年，《刀锋战士》最先上映，讲述的是一个超级英雄猎杀吸血鬼的故事。这部电影由韦斯利 · 斯奈普斯主演，在全球获得了一亿三千一百万美元的票房。第一部《X 战警》电影于 2000 年上映，票房更高。影评人很喜欢这部电影，观众纷纷拥向影院。《X 战警》的票房为两亿美元。这部电影也是斯坦第一次出演的漫威电影。他在里面扮演了一个热狗推销员！两年后，《蜘蛛侠》终于上映了。这部电影由托比 · 马奎尔饰演彼得 · 帕克，威廉 · 达福饰演绿魔，克里斯汀 · 邓斯特饰演玛丽 · 简 · 沃森。它在全球范围内大获成功，获得了八亿两千两百万美元的票房收入！

X战警

在好莱坞奋斗了二十年后，斯坦终于看到他的漫威梦梦想成真了。

斯坦·李饰演过的电影角色

斯坦·李是一位留着白色小胡子的绅士，他在许多超级英雄电影中都只出现过一分钟。斯坦在里面“客串”。“客串”通常是指一个名人扮演一个非常小的角色。以下是斯坦最著名的几次客串：

《神奇四侠》——邮递员威利·伦普金（斯坦在《神奇四侠》漫画书里创造的一个角色）

《X战警》——热狗推销员

《绿巨人》——保安

《钢铁侠3》——选美大赛评委

《蜘蛛侠3》——看滚动字幕的老爷爷（他甚至还说了一句他最喜欢的台词：“不说了。”）

《雷神：黑暗世界》——精神病院的一个病人

斯坦喜欢蜘蛛侠，但漫威最成功的电影还在后头。

《钢铁侠》于 2008 年上映，小罗伯特 · 唐尼饰演了一个身家过亿的冒险家托尼 · 斯塔克。斯坦认为小罗伯特 · 唐尼天生就是演斯塔克的料！这个演员非常适合这个角色。《钢铁侠》大获成功，后来又出了两部续集。

小罗伯特 · 唐尼

2013 年,《钢铁侠 3》在全球赚了十二亿美元!

“我认为漫威最终会成为娱乐圈最大的公司。”斯坦在接受采访时说。

第九章

精神永存

有些人老了就退休了。他们会打打高尔夫球或乘船游览。斯坦则不是这样。

“我认为，如果你喜欢你所做的事情，那就像玩游戏一样，根本停不下来，”他在接受采访时表示，“会乐在其中。”他说这话的时候已经八十九岁了！

虽然斯坦在20世纪90年代就辞去了漫威发行人的职务，但他在许多以他创造的角色为主角的电影中都担任了执行制片人。并不是说他需要这份工作。创造了一些世界上最受欢迎的漫画人物后，他已经非常富有了。

但斯坦从不过分关心钱的问题。他喜欢创造出新点子。随着年龄的增长，他开始不断尝试新事物。他甚至

还为竞争对手工作！多年来，DC 漫画一直是漫威最大的竞争对手。2001 年，DC 漫画公司请斯坦创作以 DC 超级英雄为主角的故事。斯坦的“试想一下”系列包括超人、蝙蝠侠、神奇女侠和其他 DC 角色。

斯坦·李

“只要我一直忙着，”他写道，“就不会过多地关注过去。”

天啊，斯坦真是忙得不可开交！他创建了其他公司，开设了自己的油管频道，并解说了一系列电子游戏。他还经常出现在漫画大会上。事实上，只要他出现，门票马上就会售罄！斯坦是一个活生生的传奇。到目前为止，数以百万计的人看过有漫威角色的漫画书或电影。漫威甚至为斯坦·李创造了一个动作人偶。

斯坦热爱他的工作，也很珍惜他的家庭。

琼·西利娅与她的父母关系很好。人们经常看到她

和父亲一起在电影首映礼上走红毯。

斯坦和他的弟弟拉里继续合作制作蜘蛛侠，每天都

有数百家报纸的漫画版面上印刷着这个版本的蜘蛛侠。

斯坦的成就远不止于此。2010 年，他开始主持自己的电视节目《斯坦·李的超人》。在他刚过九十岁生日之后的一次采访中，他兴奋地谈到了漫威未来的计划，提到了《奇异博士》《蚁人》和《银河护卫队》等电影。

遗憾的是，李不得不取消在丹佛举行的漫画大会上的演出。但这并不是因为他太累或年龄太大了。那是因为好莱坞需要他。《超凡蜘蛛侠 2》正在拍摄，斯坦是时候客串下一个角色了。

就像斯坦说的：“还有什么比这更有趣呢？”

斯坦·李

斯坦 · 李生平年表

1922 年 — 斯坦 · 李在纽约出生。

1939 年 — 斯坦成为时代漫画公司的助理。

1941 年 — 斯坦的第一个漫画故事出现在《美国队长》系列漫画的第三部里。同年，斯坦接任《时代漫画》杂志的总编。

1942 年 — 斯坦应征入伍。

1945 年 — 斯坦服完兵役后，回到了时代漫画公司。

1947 年 — 斯坦与琼 · 克莱顿 · 布科克结婚。

1950 年 — 斯坦和琼的女儿琼 · 西利娅（J.C.）出生。

1951 年 — 时代漫画公司更名为亚特拉斯漫画公司。

1961 年 — 斯坦和杰克 · 科比创造了神奇四侠，他们的第一个超级英雄团队。亚特拉斯漫画更名为漫威漫画。

1965 年 — 斯坦发布漫威的“牛棚公告”，其中的专栏《斯坦的肥皂箱》里面刊载了他写给读者的公开信。

1971 年 — 在美国政府的要求下，斯坦同意创作包含反毒品信息的蜘蛛侠故事线。

1980 年 — 斯坦搬到洛杉矶为漫威漫画制作电影。

1994 年 — 斯坦被列入威尔 · 艾斯纳名人堂，是为漫画创作者设立的一个特别荣誉。

1998 年 — 由韦斯利 · 斯奈普斯主演的《刀锋战士》成为漫威第一部大热电影。

2000 年 — 第一部《X 战警》电影上映。

2002 年 — 第一部《蜘蛛侠》电影上映，随后上映了《蜘蛛侠 2》（2004）、《蜘蛛侠 3》（2007）和《超凡蜘蛛侠》（2012）。

2008 年 — 第一部《钢铁侠》电影上映，随后上映了《钢铁侠 2》（2010）和《钢铁侠 3》（2013）。

2010 年 — 纪录片《斯坦 · 李的故事：真正的信仰者》上映。

2018 年 — 11 月 12 日逝世，享年 95 岁。

世界大事记

1929 年 — 股票市场崩盘，引发了经济大萧条。

1941 年 — 日本偷袭美国珍珠港军事基地，美国加入第二次世界大战。

1945 年 — 第二次世界大战结束。

1947 年 — 杰基 · 罗宾逊成为第一位在美国职棒大联盟打球的非裔美国人。

1956 年 — 埃尔维斯 · 普雷斯利的《伤心旅馆》成为他的第一首金曲。

1969 年 — 尼尔 · 阿姆斯特朗登月，成为月球漫步第一人。

1972 年 — HBO 成为第一个付费电视频道。

1975 年 — 越南战争结束。

1984 年 — 苹果公司发布了第一台麦金塔个人电脑。

1997 年 — “哈利 · 波特” 系列第一本小说出版。

2001 年 — 苹果公司发布了第一代 iPod 音乐播放器。

2004 年 — 马克 · 扎克伯格和一群朋友创建了脸书（Facebook）。

Who Was Stan Lee?

Martin Goodman, the publisher of Timely Comics in New York City, didn't know what to do with the teenager. But the boy was his wife's cousin and she had asked Goodman to hire him. So, just like that, Stanley Martin Lieber was working in the middle of the Golden Age of Comics. As a boy, Stan spent hours curled up with comic books. Now, he was part of that world!

Superheroes were everywhere at Timely. The Human Torch fought bad guys with fire. Namor the Sub-Mariner could fly and breathe underwater, and he was as strong as a thousand men. Captain America began life as a scrawny art student, but turned into a superhero after the US government recruited him for the Super Soldier project.

At first, Stan kept to himself. The artists at Timely

were a little scary. They were all older, smoked big cigars, and yelled at each other all day long. What was there for a sixteen-year-old kid from the Bronx to do?

Young Stanley Lieber ran to the deli for sandwiches at lunchtime and made sure the artists' inkwells were full. But he wasn't going to waste a lifetime fetching coffee and answering phones. He had dreams. He was a writer. He wanted to tell stories and maybe someday write the great American novel.

One day, two of Timely Comics' top managers both got angry and quit their jobs. Mr. Goodman needed someone to run the office while he was taking naps or playing golf. He called Stan over and offered him the job.

That's when Stanley Lieber became Stan Lee. In the next half century, he would help create some of America's most famous superheroes, including Spider-Man, Iron Man,

Hulk, and the X-Men. He wasn't the only person who made comic books for a living, but Stan Lee was the best.

Chapter 1

Growing Up

Stanley Lieber was born on December 28, 1922, in New York City.

His father, Jack, and mother, Celia, were immigrants from Romania who lived in a tiny apartment. Like millions of people, they had come to the United States with dreams of a better life. They wanted to start a family and buy a house.

Jack got a job cutting fabric at a dress factory. He was paid very little and worked long hours. Celia stayed home and took care of Stan. By the time Stanley was six, the Great Depression had begun. Millions of people lost their jobs, including Stan's father.

Now the family struggled to pay bills. Jack and Celia

began to argue. Stan worried whenever his parents argued. He loved his parents and didn't want them to fight.

The Lieber family moved to an even smaller apartment. Jack and Celia had to sleep on a cot in the living room. There was only one tiny window, and it faced a brick wall.

Stan's mother wanted him to finish school quickly so he could go to work to help the family. She pushed Stan to study hard, and he did. He ended up skipping a few grades, which meant that he was always the youngest in his class. He sometimes struggled to make friends.

Stan's favorite teacher was Leon B. Ginsberg, Jr. Mr. Ginsberg had a great sense of humor and always told a funny story to make his point. Stan learned that people remember stories if they are told with a sense of humor.

As a boy, Stan loved to write. He also loved to read—even if it was just the label of a ketchup bottle on the kitchen table! In fact, Stan always had a book or magazine with him at meals. The Hardy Boys was one of his favorite book

The Great Depression

The Great Depression started on October 29, 1929, when the stock market crashed, causing many banks and industries to shut down. It was the worst economic crisis of modern times. Unemployment peaked in 1933, when one-quarter of all Americans were out of work and could not find jobs.

President Herbert Hoover' s name became linked to the hardships that many people faced. "Hoovervilles"—towns made up of tents and shacks built by people who had no other place to live—popped up everywhere. Soup was called "Hoover Stew."

The Great Depression lasted nearly ten years. It affected not only the United States but countries all around the world.

series. Two adventurous brothers, Frank and Joe Hardy, were the heroes of the books. Stan also loved to draw. He wasn't the best artist, but that didn't matter. Drawing helped Stan tell his stories.

During the summers, many New York boys went to camps outside the city. But the Liebers couldn't afford to send Stan away to camp. Instead, Stan stayed home and read. Stan's mother even bought him a stand to keep his books upright on the table while he ate.

Whenever he could afford a ticket, Stan loved to go to the movies. There were five theaters to choose from near his apartment. They showed movies like *Frankenstein, Sherlock Holmes*, and *King Kong*. Stan daydreamed of being like Errol Flynn, the handsome actor who starred as Robin Hood.

When Stan was nine, his brother, Larry, was born. As Stan got older, the family really needed him to pitch in and get a job.

Stan was not afraid of hard work. He took any job

Young Stan's Favorite Authors

H. G. Wells (1866-1946) grew up in England and was known as "The Father of Science Fiction." His most famous book, *The War of the Worlds*, was about the world being taken over by aliens. Wells wrote it long before people had cars, or could even imagine building rockets for space travel.

Mark Twain (1835-1910) was an American from Missouri. His books about Tom Sawyer and Huckleberry Finn were written the way people actually spoke. He also wrote about how white people were prejudiced against blacks. This was revolutionary at the time.

Sir Arthur Conan Doyle (1859-1930) was from Scotland and created the amazing detective Sherlock Holmes. Holmes smoked a pipe and solved mysteries with his best friend, Dr. Watson.

he could get. He wrote for a news company. He delivered sandwiches. And he worked in the office of a company that made pants.

Even as he worked to help his family, Stan kept writing. And he was getting good at it. A local newspaper sponsored a writing contest. Stan won so many times, the newspaper asked him to stop entering! They wanted someone else to have a chance to win. But the newspaper editor also praised Stan and urged him to do something with his talent. That kind of encouragement meant a lot. Stan would never forget it.

Chapter 2

Becoming Stan Lee

In 1939, when Stan was just sixteen, he graduated from DeWitt Clinton High School. Many kids his age were thinking about college. Not Stan. He needed to keep working. With the help of his cousin Jean, he got a job at Timely, a publishing company run by Martin Goodman.

Mr. Goodman barely knew Stan. "What are you doing here?" Mr. Goodman asked Stan when he showed up for work.

Was Mr. Goodman joking? Had Jean forgotten to mention Stan to her husband? He never got a chance to find out. He was too busy.

Timely published more than two dozen magazines out of

its Manhattan offices. Some featured adventure stories set in the Old West; others were about science and health. Stan was assigned to Timely's comics department. "Some department," Stan joked. "It was Joe and Jack."

Joe was Joe Simon. He was the top editor—the man in charge of all the words on the page. Jack was Jack Kirby. He was the best artist at Timely. These two men were big influences on Stan. But they weren't friendly. When Stan first arrived, they barely looked up.

In those first days on the job, Stan worked as a "gofer"—somebody who does whatever the boss needs. Though he was paid only eight dollars a week, Stan didn't mind. He was proud to be working at Timely.

Stan commuted every day from the Bronx down to Timely's offices on Forty-Second Street. The room Joe and Jack worked in was nothing special. Jack would sit at his drawing board. Joe would pace around the room. Stan sometimes joked that he couldn't see them through all the cigar smoke.

At that time, there was fierce competition from other comic-book companies. DC Comics had created Superman and Batman. Timely's two superheroes were less famous.

The Human Torch was an android created in a lab. He had the power to shoot fire from his hands. He could suddenly burst into flames. But he could not always control those flames. The Sub-Mariner had an even bigger problem. He was the son of a human sea captain and a princess from Atlantis, and he didn't seem to like humans at all!

In 1940, Joe Simon and Jack Kirby created Captain America for Timely Comics. World War II was raging in Europe, and Simon and Kirby were horrified by what they had heard about Adolf Hitler. Captain America's mission was to fight Nazi Germany. He wore a red, white, and blue costume, the same colors as the American flag. He carried a shield that could stop bullets.

The first issue was a huge success. It sold a million

How Comics Are Made

A comic book is put together in five main stages. The writer creates the story. The penciler illustrates the story in pencil sketches. Then a letterer carefully prints all the words of the story onto the page in ink. At every stage, the editor makes sure the work is good enough to go to the next step.

When ready, the pages go to the inker. These days, a computer often creates thick ink lines over the finished pencil drawings. The comic- book companies can save money by using a computer instead of a person. But even into the 1990s, the inker was an important artist. His or her job was to turn pencil drawings into dramatic black-and-white comic art.

After the pencils are inked, the comic book is colored and then printed.

copies. Superman had competition!

That's when Stan got a chance to do more than answer phones. One day, Joe Simon called Stan over. He asked if Stan would be able to write a story for a new issue of Captain America. Stan was thrilled! He turned in a story called "Captain America Foils the Traitor's Revenge."

Nobody said much about his first story. Stan didn't mind. All that mattered was that Stan got assigned another story right away.

After "The Traitor's Revenge," Stan began to write more. As he wrote, Stan decided to use a pen name instead of his real name. He considered Headline Hunter, Foreign Correspondent, Stan Martine, and even Neels Nats, which was almost "Stan Lee" spelled backward! Stan didn't want to use his full name, Stanley Lieber. "I was saving that for the great American novel," he joked later, "which I never wrote." Finally, he settled on a permanent pen name—Stan Lee—both his names, cut in half.

Chapter 3

The Teenager Takes Over

As Stan was assigned more writing jobs, Joe and Jack were assigned fewer. Mr. Goodman could be difficult. He didn't like to pay the artists much, and they were not happy about it. So Joe and Jack decided to quit.

"I looked around to see who would replace them and I realized, there was nobody," Stan said later. "I was the only guy there."

Stan had lots of ideas for stories, but couldn't draw well. So he worked closely with the artists. He also continued as the company's editor, though it was sometimes hard to be an eighteen-year-old boss. Some days, Stan would answer the office door and be asked, "Hey, kid, where can I find Mr.

Lee?"

For about a year, Stan ran Timely and wrote whatever Mr. Goodman wanted. He wrote westerns, mysteries, and horror, and even some romance stories. As much as Stan loved his job, he was distracted. The United States had entered World War II, and Stan wanted to do his part.

He decided to volunteer for the army and reported for duty in the winter of 1942.

Stan's military classification was "playwright." Because of his work experience, Stan was given a job writing slogans, manuals, and training films for the US government. This was a rare assignment. Only eight other people have ever been classified as "playwright" by the US Army, including film director Frank Capra, novelist William Saroyan, and Theodor Geisel, better known as Dr. Seuss.

Remarkably, Stan kept working for Timely while he was in the army. The company would mail Stan ideas, and he would send finished stories back to them from wherever he was stationed. As much as Stan liked serving his country, he was thrilled when the war ended in 1945. He couldn’t wait to get back to the world of comic books.

World War II

The Second World War was the biggest war in history. It officially began in 1939 in Europe. Every major country in the world was involved, with one hundred million people around the world serving in military units. Two opposing military alliances were formed: the Allies and the Axis.

The United States joined the war after a surprise attack by Japanese bombers on Pearl Harbor, Hawaii, on December 7, 1941. Nearly 2,400 servicemen died that day.

Pearl Harbor terrified Americans. But it also inspired them. Men volunteered to go overseas and join the Allies (which included England, France, and the Soviet Union) to fight the Axis (which included Germany, Italy, and Japan).

Even though the Allied Forces won the war, the victory came at a great price. More than fifty million people died before Germany and Japan finally surrendered in 1945, making World War II the deadliest conflict in human history.

Chapter 4

Joanie

When World War II ended, Stan returned to New York to take over again as Timely's editor. It was a job he would keep for over twenty-five years, until 1972 when he became publisher. Stan was having the time of his life. He rented a two-room apartment in the Almanac Hotel and bought a big white car. It was the first brand-new car he had ever owned!

Then things got even better. A friend wanted to introduce Stan to a model named Betty. His friend thought that Betty and Stan would make a great couple. When Stan showed up at the modeling agency, the most beautiful woman he had ever seen answered the door. There was only one problem: She wasn't Betty. She was a young woman named Joan.

Joan Clayton Boocock had red hair and blue eyes and a great sense of humor. She had moved from England to New York to work as a hat model. In the 1940s, women wore hats every day. And hat models had to be beautiful. Their faces were featured in advertisements in newspapers and magazines.

Stan wasn't one to hold back his feelings. "I love you," he blurted out that first day. Joan laughed. But she agreed to go on a date.

On December 5, 1947, Stan and Joan became husband and wife. They were married by the same judge who had granted Joan a divorce from her first husband just moments before! Stan wanted to marry Joan quickly, before she could change her mind!

Stan was thrilled and called his beautiful new bride Joanie.

The young couple moved to an apartment close to Timely's offices in Manhattan. The place was so small it barely fit more than their bed. But Stan and Joanie didn't mind. They spent nights out dancing with their friends. Life was great.

Two years later, Stan and Joan moved to a house on Long Island, just outside of New York City. When Stan's mother, Celia, died, his younger brother, Larry, was only fifteen years old. He moved into the new house with Stan and Joanie.

And it's a good thing they had much more space! In 1950, Stan and Joan had a baby girl, Joan Celia. They were heartbroken three years later when a second daughter, Jan, died a few days after she was born. The doctors told Joanie she couldn't have any more children.

Stan loved their daughter, "J.C." He would put her on his shoulders and carry her around their big yard. He took pictures of her with their loving German shepherds, Blackie and Simba. And, in order to spend more time with J.C., Stan tried to work at home as much as possible.

Happy not to be cooped up in Timely's smoke-filled offices, Stan would work outside in the sun. He put his typewriter on a backyard table and worked while standing up. Sometimes, friends would come over and keep Stan company. At other times, J.C. would have her own young friends over to the house.

It was difficult not to notice Stan when he was hard at work. While he wrote comic books, Stan liked to read all the words out loud. It helped him make his superheroes sound right. *Pow! Zap!* He would shout all the most dramatic parts!

J.C.'s friends sometimes wondered why her father was making all that noise. J.C. told them not to worry. That was just her father at work.

Chapter 5

Comics Under Attack

Not everybody loved comics as much as Stan did. Starting in the early 1940s, some adults complained that comic books were bad for children. Why? They were filled with violence, bloody details, and horrific stories. People were afraid that comics would influence young people in dangerous ways.

In 1948, angry parents even held public comic-book burnings in Binghamton, New York, and Spencer, West Virginia. And in 1949, the very popular *Family Circle* magazine published a story called "What Can You Do about Comic Books?" The article told parents they needed to read comic books before their children did to make sure they were "safe" and not too violent.

Stan and the other comic-book creators didn't take the complaints very seriously. Business was still very good.

But in 1954, Fredric Wertham, a child psychologist, wrote a book called *Seduction of the Innocent*. Dr. Wertham said that comics were dangerous to children. His ideas led to congressional hearings in Washington, DC, about whether to outlaw comic books. Some stores even stopped selling them to children!

The congressional hearings had a huge impact on sales. Fifteen comic-book companies went out of business in 1954 alone.

The remaining publishers did their best to survive. Together, they founded the Comics Code Authority. They wrote their own rules to make sure comic books didn't include stories that would upset parents or politicians. The Comics Code Authority had to approve every comic book before it was printed. If approved, the comic could use the Comics Code Seal of Approval on its front cover. That meant it was "safe" for children to read.

The Comics Code Authority

The Comics Code Authority established that comic books would:

· show respect for authority (such as the police).

· ensure that good would always triumph over evil.

· not use the words "terror" or "horror."

· show no vampires, werewolves, ghouls, or zombies!

Stan followed the code for years. In 1971, the US government asked Stan to create a Spider-Man comic about the dangers of drugs and drug use. But the Comics Code Authority didn't allow comic books to even mention drugs! Stan ignored the Code and published three anti-drug issues featuring Spider-Man. They didn't get a seal of approval. Still, the comics were a hit. Stan now knew he could make his own rules. In 2001, Marvel did just that, officially withdrawing from the Comics Code Authority and creating its own rating system.

Chapter 6

Marvel Is Born

By 1960, Stan had been working on comic books for twenty years. But he really wasn't having much fun anymore. Comic books were not selling. Kids were more interested in television shows and rock-and-roll music than old superheroes. Even Captain America was canceled due to low sales.

Stan couldn't help thinking of the good old days with Jack Kirby in the smoky rooms at Timely. He missed the old team and the excitement he used to feel when he came to work. He told Joanie that he was going to quit. He was planning to stomp into Mr. Goodman's office and tell him that he was through with comics.

There was only one problem.

Just when he was ready to quit, Mr. Goodman offered Stan an exciting new challenge. A rival company, DC Comics, had just put out a comic book: the *Justice League of America.* Instead of just one superhero, the comic book included seven of them working as a team: Superman, Batman, Wonder Woman, Flash, Green Lantern, Aquaman, and the Martian Manhunter!

Justice League comics were flying off the shelf.

Mr. Goodman asked Stan to create his own team. He even suggested bringing back Captain America and the Human Torch.

When Stan told Joanie about Mr. Goodman's idea, she told Stan that she would always support him. She knew her husband better than anybody. She knew he loved a creative challenge.

"You know, Stan," Joanie said, "if Martin wants you to create a new group of superheroes, this could be a chance for you to do it in a way you've always wanted to."

By that, she meant that Stan had nothing to lose. If he took too much of a risk and annoyed Mr. Goodman, he might get fired. That wouldn't matter to Stan because he had already planned to quit! But if he came up with something special, he might please Mr. Goodman and recapture the excitement of his early days at Timely.

Stan didn't want to just bring back old characters. He wanted to create new ones. His new team would not be perfectly handsome like Superman or incredibly strong like Captain America. They would have the normal problems and weaknesses of regular people. Their lives would not always be easy.

And Stan knew exactly who could help: his old partner Jack.

It had been years since Jack had quit his regular job at Timely Comics. But starting in 1958, Jack had been taking assignments from Stan. Now, Stan needed something more. He needed Jack's help in creating a new generation of comic-book heroes.

The Fantastic Four were led by the brilliant scientist Reed Richards. Sue Storm hoped to marry Reed one day. Sue's younger brother, Johnny Storm, was the third member of the team. But Stan and Jack's greatest creation was the final member of the Fantastic Four: Ben Grimm. Ben was a military pilot who was a friend of Reed's.

It was Reed's dream to travel to outer space. He built a spacecraft and invited Ben, Sue, and Johnny along. Once in space, they were blasted by radiation, which gave each of them special powers. But Ben became deformed. The radiation turned him into a giant creature with an orange, rock-like skin. Depressed, Ben renamed himself The Thing.

The Thing was a new kind of superhero. He grumbled and rolled his eyes. He wished he could go back to being his normal self. But he was incredibly loyal and also believed in fighting crime. Reed became the bigmouthed Mr. Fantastic. Sue Storm became the Invisible Girl. Johnny Storm, who

Jack Kirby

Jack Kirby was born on August 28, 1917. When he was just fourteen, he began taking classes at art school. Soon after, he had to quit school when his father lost his job.

Jack was a very good artist. At Timely and later at Marvel Comics, Jack helped create Captain America, The Fantastic Four, and other important superheroes. They called him "King" Kirby. But Jack didn't like nicknames. He liked getting credit for his work. He thought that Stan hogged the spotlight, and he grew bitter about not being given enough attention for the characters he created. He wondered why so many articles mentioned only Stan.

Stan told everyone that Jack had created the characters with him. But by the time he died in 1994, Jack felt cheated and hadn't talked to Stan for years.

Jack Kirby is remembered as one of the greatest comic-book artists of all time.

could now burst into flames at will, became the new Human Torch.

When the first comic book was published in 1961, readers loved the Fantastic Four! Their success convinced Stan that he had made the right decision to take on Mr. Goodman's challenge. It also gave him the confidence to create other unlikely heroes.

As a boy, Stan had read Robert Louis Stevenson's *The Strange Case of Dr. Jekyll and Mr. Hyde*. The book told the story of one man with two very different personalities. Dr. Jekyll was a very good person, but as Mr. Hyde, he was evil.

For the new character, Stan came up with his own version of Dr. Jekyll and Mr. Hyde. Dr. Bruce Banner was a mild-mannered scientist. But when he lost his temper or felt panicked, he turned into a green monster: the Hulk.

The Hulk first appeared in 1962 in *The Incredible Hulk #1* and became instantly popular among comic-book fans.

Stan's next comic team was a group of outcast mutants

called the X-Men. Professor Xavier, their mentor, showed them that they also could be heroes.

Stan was on a roll, but was very busy and needed help. He had the perfect guy for the job. He called in his younger brother, Larry. Larry Lieber had gone to art school and done some writing for Stan. Now they began to work together more closely. Over the next two years, Stan and Larry would help create two of their most popular characters, Thor and Iron Man. When Larry got tired of drawing those characters, he launched a western series called Rawhide Kid. Stan kept coming up with new characters, including Daredevil and Ant-Man.

With so much success, Stan decided to make a big change.

In the 1950s, Mr. Goodman had changed Timely's name to Atlas Comics. But Stan had thought the company needed a fresher name. Times were changing. Stan was developing comics with a new style and approach. Although he had gone back to using superheroes, this new wave of crime fighters was different. They had issues! They sometimes struggled with their superpowers and longed for their days as mere humans. Stan remembered the title used in one of the early comic books published by Timely: Marvel. He liked the sound of that! And Mr. Goodman agreed.

Stan gave his crew of artists and writers at Marvel Comics nicknames and called the team his " bullpen. " The writers, artists, and inkers worked in the main room at Marvel. Stan wanted Marvel's readers to imagine the company as a big clubhouse where everybody hung out, told jokes, and developed amazing comic books.

If readers had a question, they could send a letter directly to Stan. He would answer those letters on a page he put in every comic book called "Bullpen Bulletins." Stan had fun writing these pages. He gave each Bulletin a funny-sounding title at the top of the page, like "More mirthful, monumental, mind-staggering memoranda from your Marvel madmen!" Stan wrote an open letter to readers called "Stan's Soapbox" and came up with his own favorite terms, like "nuff said" and "Excelsior!"

Other comic-book companies were "Brand *Echh*," Stan joked. Marvel Comics was king.

M.M.M.S.

Marvel Comics' in-house fan club was launched in February 1965. Called the "Merry Marvel Marching Society" (or M.M.M.S., for short), the club included various ranks such as Q. N. S. (Quite 'Nuff Sayer) and F.F.F. (Fearless Front-Facer). For the one-dollar membership fee, club members would receive a welcome letter, a membership card, stickers, buttons, and a one-sided record called *The Voices of Marvel* featuring Stan, the guys of the bullpen, and Stan's secretary, "Fabulous Flo" Steinberg.

In 1969, the M.M.M.S. was absorbed into the larger fan club, Marvelmania International.

Chapter 7

Spider-Man

Even with the company's new name and newfound success, Stan had trouble explaining his latest idea to Mr. Goodman. Who would be interested in a skinny teenager who could stick to ceilings like a fly? "Spider-Man"? Didn't Stan realize that people hated spiders?

Stan said he came up with the idea for Spider-Man after watching a fly climb up a wall. How about a superhero who could stick to things? Stan struggled to come up with a good name. Fly-Man or Insect-Man didn't sound right. Then, Stan thought of Spider-Man. That could work!

He originally wanted to ask artist Jack Kirby to draw the new character, but decided that Jack's drawings were not right. Jack made Spider-Man look too heroic, too powerful.

Spider-Man was really Peter Parker, a geeky teenager who was unsure of himself. He got pushed around in school by a football star named Flash Thompson. Then a radioactive spider bit Peter and gave him special powers. The shy boy could suddenly stick to walls and ceilings as if he had suction cups for hands. He was also super strong.

To create this new superhero, Stan found an artistic partner in Steve Ditko. Steve himself was awkward and shy and didn't like to go to parties. He had no problem making Peter Parker different. He would not be a giant, muscle-bound hero. But when Peter transformed into Spider-Man, he was drawn like a classic superhero, with a new "look" and costume designed by Steve.

Spider-Man first appeared in a comic book in June 1962, and he was the perfect character for Stan's new approach: regular people who happen to become superheroes. The Marvel characters would have flaws and problems. But ultimately, they would devote themselves to fighting crime.

Despite Mr. Goodman's doubts, the first comic book to feature Spider-Man was popular. In fact, Marvel's new group of superheroes sold thirteen million comic books in 1962—nearly double the amount they sold the previous year!

Stan had been part of the "Golden Age of Comics" in the 1940s. Now he was part creator of the "Silver Age," which lasted roughly from 1956-1970. Comic fans sometimes refer to this popular return to superheroes—and away from crime and romance stories—as the "Silver Sixties" and even "The Marvel Age."

Who said nobody likes spiders?

Some of Marvel's Biggest Villains

Doctor Doom is an inventor and a sorcerer who is the archenemy of The Fantastic Four.

Galactus, from the planet Taa, is so powerful he can eat entire planets.

The Green Goblin, one of Spider-Man's enemies, is a Halloween-themed supervillain whose weapons include bats, ghosts, and exploding jack-o-lanterns.

Ultron's outer armor is so powerful, he is almost indestructible. He is also a genius.

Thanos is a mutant who can travel through space with a special chair. He uses his superhuman strength to battle Iron Man, The Thing, and Spider-Man.

Loki is both Thor's adopted brother—and his sworn enemy. His full name is Loki Laufeyson.

Venom, a liquid-like alien looking for a human host, is one of Spider-Man's archenemies.

Magneto was born on Earth with special powers. He became a villain after his family died during World War II and he decided mutants needed to be defended.

Onslaught was created from the combined souls of Professor X and Magneto. he battles both the Hulk and the X-Men.

Chapter 8

Movie Stardom for Marvel

With Marvel Comics now making so much money, Mr. Goodman decided it was time to sell. A man named Martin Ackerman bought the company in 1968 with one condition: Stan Lee had to remain in charge.

Stan did. By now, Stan was the face of Marvel. While the artists tended to keep to themselves, Stan's outgoing nature made him a natural spokesman for the company. He spoke at colleges and conventions. He posed for magazines and newspapers. Stan also had developed his distinctive look. He grew an identifiable mustache and always wore sunglasses, even when he was inside!

In 1972, when Mr. Goodman officially retired as

publisher, Stan got a promotion. He became the publisher of Marvel. Roy Thomas, a writer who had been working on X-Men, became Marvel's editor. As publisher, Stan could focus on new ideas.

Stan wanted the Marvel characters to branch out into television shows and movies.

Television was easy. In 1977, *The Incredible Hulk* made its premiere on TV. Stan was not in charge of the show, but he did have an important role. The producers of *The Incredible Hulk* wanted the Hulk to be red, not green. Stan said no. The Hulk had to be green. *The Incredible Hulk* ran for more than eighty episodes over five years!

Stan had a tougher time getting Marvel into the movies. For years, movie producers had refused to turn comic books into movies. They worried that it would be too difficult to show illustrated comic-book action using real actors. In 1978, everything changed when the movie *Superman* came out. Actor Christopher Reeve played Superman. The movie earned $300 million worldwide, the sixth highest-grossing film ever at that time. *Superman* convinced Hollywood that superhero movies could work.

Stan began to meet with Hollywood producers, and in 1980, he and Joanie moved to Los Angeles. They bought a house in West Hollywood overlooking the Sunset Strip, a glamorous part of the city full of stores, restaurants, and rock clubs. It was so exciting! Stan and Joanie loved Hollywood. They made new friends in California. J.C. worked as a model and began painting. Her parents were thrilled to go to her first art show.

As much as Stan loved California, he found it wasn't easy to get movies made. Producers argued. They sued each other. At one point writers had written eight different scripts for a movie version of Spider-Man. Nobody was satisfied.

Director James Cameron wanted to make a Spider-Man movie. But it was taking too long. He made movies like *Terminator* and *Titanic* instead.

In 1989, a movie about Marvel's character the Punisher was filmed, but never released in movie theaters. Neither was 1994's version of the Fantastic Four.

The struggles in Hollywood caught Stan by surprise. Back in New York, Marvel Comics was also having problems. Ackerman had sold Marvel in 1986, and the new owners wanted to expand. The company tried to get too big, too fast. They bought a baseball-card company and a sticker company. Both lost money.

Finally, in 1996, Marvel went bankrupt. The company was broke.

But Stan never gave up. He knew the Marvel family of characters would someday find new fans on the big screen. He also knew that Marvel needed him. Everybody knew Stan Lee! To relaunch Marvel, the new owners came up with a plan.

They created a department within Marvel that was devoted exclusively to making movies. They called it Marvel

Studios. A man named Avi Arad was put in charge. Avi had grown up in Israel reading Spider-Man comic books translated into Hebrew. He was thrilled to have Stan giving him advice.

With Avi in charge, Marvel finally began to get films made. *Blade* came first, in 1998, based on a superhero who hunted vampires. The movie starred Wesley Snipes and earned $131 million around the world.

The first X-Men movie came out in 2000 and was even bigger. Critics loved it, and crowds flocked to theaters. *X-Men* earned $200 million. The film also featured Stan's first appearance in a Marvel film. He played a hot-dog salesman! Two years later, *Spider-Man* was finally released. The movie starred Tobey Maguire as Peter Parker, Willem Dafoe as the Green Goblin, and Kirsten Dunst as Mary Jane Watson. It was a worldwide hit, earning $822 million!

After twenty years in Hollywood, Stan was finally seeing his dreams for Marvel come true.

Stan Lee's Movie Roles

The distinguished gentleman with the white mustache who appears for just a minute in so many superhero movies is Stan Lee. Stan appears in what is called a "cameo" role. A cameo usually involves somebody famous playing a very tiny role. Here are a few of Stan's most famous cameos:

Fantastic Four—Willie Lumpkin, the mailman (a character Stan had created for the Fantastic Four comic books)

X-Men—hot-dog vendor

Hulk—security guard

Iron Man 3—beauty pageant judge

Spider-Man 3—man reading a news ticker. (He even gets to say one of his favorite lines, "Nuff said.")

Thor: The Dark World—patient in a mental hospital

Stan loved *Spider-Man*, but Marvel's biggest movie success was still to come.

Iron Man came out in 2008, with Robert Downey Jr. starring as the billionaire adventurer Tony Stark. Stan thought Robert Downey Jr. was born to play Stark! The actor was perfect for the role. *Iron Man* was such a smash, it led to two sequels. In 2013, *Iron Man 3* earned $1.2 billion around the world, making it the fifth highest-grossing film of all time!

"I think Marvel will end up being the biggest company in showbiz," Stan said in an interview.

Chapter 9

Legacy

Some people retire when they get older. They pick up their golf clubs or take a cruise. Not Stan.

"I think if you enjoy what you do it's like playing and you can't stop," he told an interviewer. "It's so much fun." He was eighty-nine when he said that!

Though Stan stepped down as Marvel's publisher in the 1990s, he continues to serve as an executive producer of the many movies that feature his characters. Not that he needs the work. Creating some of the world's most popular comic-book characters has made him very rich.

But Stan was never overly concerned with money. He loved dreaming up new ideas. As he got older, he tried new things. He even went to work for the competition! For years, DC Comics was Marvel's biggest rival. In 2001, DC Comics asked Stan to write stories featuring the DC superheroes. Stan's *Just Imagine . . .* series included Superman, Batman, Wonder Woman, and other DC characters.

"As long as I can keep busy," he wrote, "it saves me from dwelling too much on the past."

And boy, has Stan kept busy! He's created other companies, started his own YouTube channel, and narrated a series of video games. He also makes appearances regularly at comic conventions. In fact, whenever he's appearing, tickets sell out within minutes! Stan is a living legend. By now, millions of people have read comic books or seen movies starring his characters. Marvel has even created a Stan Lee action figure.

Stan loves his work and he cherishes his family. J.C. has stayed close to her parents. She is often seen walking down the red carpet with her father at movie premieres.

Stan and his younger brother, Larry, continue to work together on the version of Spider-Man that is printed on the comics page in hundreds of newspapers each day.

Stan's work is far from done. In 2010, he started hosting his own television show, *Stan Lee's Superhumans*. And in an interview just after his ninetieth birthday, he got excited as he talked about future Marvel plans, mentioning movies about Doctor Strange, Ant-Man, and Guardians of the Galaxy.

Lee regrettably had to cancel a sold-out appearance at a comics convention in Denver. But it wasn't because he was too tired or too old. It was because Hollywood needed him. *The Amazing Spider-Man 2* was filming, and it was time for Stan's next cameo.

As Stan would say, "What could be more fun?"

Timeline of Stan Lee's Life

1922	Stanley Lieber is born in New York City.
1939	Stan joins Timely Comics as an assistant.
1941	Stan's first comic-book story appears in *Captain America Comics #3*. Later that year, Stan takes over as editor at Timely.
1942	Stan joins the US Army.
1945	Stan returns to Timely Comics after finishing his military service.
1947	Stan marries Joan Clayton Boocock.
1950	Stan and Joan's daughter Joan Celia ("J.C.") is born.
1951	Timely Comics is renamed Atlas Comics.
1961	Stan and Jack Kirby create the Fantastic Four, their first superhero team. Atlas Comics renamed Marvel Comics.
1965	Stan launches Marvel's "Bullpen Bulletins," which includes his open letter to readers, called "Stan' s Soapbox" .
1971	Stan agrees to do Spider-Man storyline with anti-drug message at request of US government.
1980	Stan moves to Los Angeles to develop movies for Marvel Comics.
1994	Stan is inducted into the Will Eisner Hall of Fame, a special honor for comic-book creators.
1998	*Blade*, starring Wesley Snipes, is Marvel's first movie hit.
2000	First *X-Men* movie is released.
2002	First *Spider-Man* movie is released, *Spider-Man 2* (2004), *Spider-Man 3* (2007), and *The Amazing Spider-Man* (2012) follow.
2008	First *Iron Man* movie is released, *Iron Man* 2 (2010) and *Iron Man 3* (2013) follow.
2010	*Stan Lee: With Great Power* documentary is released.
2018	Dies November 12, age ninety-five.

Timeline of the World

1929	Stock market crash leads to the Great Depression.
1941	Japan attacks American military base at Pearl Harbor, leading United States to enter World War II.
1945	World War II ends.
1947	Jackie Robinson becomes the first African American to play in the major leagues.
1956	Elvis Presley's "Heartbreak Hotel" becomes his first number one hit.
1969	Neil Armstrong is the first man to walk on the moon.
1972	HBO becomes the first pay-television channel.
1975	The Vietnam War comes to an end.
1984	Apple releases its first Macintosh personal computer.
1997	The first Harry Potter novel is published.
2001	Apple releases the first line of iPod music players.
2004	Mark Zuckerberg and a group of friends found Facebook.

Bibliography

Broverman, Aaron. "Stan Lee Talks the Future of Comics, Comic Book Movies and Superheroes." Moviefone.com. August 26, 2010.

Duncan, Randy, and Matthew J. Smith. The Power of Comics: History, Form and Culture. New York: Continuum, 2009.

Gitlin, Martin. Stan Lee: Comic Book Superhero (Essential Lives). Minneapolis: Abdo Publishing, 2009.

Howe, Sean. Marvel Comics: The Untold Story. New York: Harper Perennial, 2013.

Irving, Christopher. Leaping Tall Buildings: The Origins of American Comics. Brooklyn: Powerhouse, 2012.

Lee, Stan. Marvel Visionaries. New York: Marvel Comics, 2005.

Lee, Stan, and George Mair. Excelsior!: The Amazing Life of Stan Lee. New York: Touchstone, 2002.

McLaughlin, Jeff (editor). Stan Lee: Conversations (Conversations with Comic Artists). Jackson, MS: University Press of Mississippi, 2007.

Raphael, Jordan. Stan Lee and the Rise and Fall of the American Comic Book. Chicago: Chicago Review Press, 2003.

Smith, Jordan. "Marvel Might Need to Get A Little Crazy: Stan Lee Talks Future Films." Hollywood.com. September 18, 2013.